WHY DO THE CREEDS MATTER?

1. *Creeds help Christians to distinguish between essential and nonessential beliefs.* Not everyone who disagrees with you is a heretic! There are some beliefs on which Christians cannot compromise. On others, we can agree to disagree. The creeds—which focus on the essential beliefs that cannot be compromised—help us to distinguish between essential and nonessential beliefs.

2. *Creeds help Christians to focus their faith and worship on the issues that matter most.* The issues that the creeds emphasize—such as the Trinity, the character of God, the nature of Jesus, and the resurrection, for example—are the ones that the earliest Christians understood to matter most. These same beliefs can provide a unifying focus for contemporary Christians' teaching and worship.

3. *Creeds help Christians to articulate clearly how their beliefs differ from other teachings.* The apostle Peter commanded his readers always "to be ready to provide to anyone who asks a defense for the hope that is in you" (1 Peter 3:15-16). When it comes to giving a defense for our faith, the creeds are crucial! When someone asks what Christians believe about the resurrection of Jesus, the Apostles' and Nicene Creeds provide concise summaries of this core doctrine. When a child in Sunday school asks why Jesus came to earth, a teacher who remembers the Nicene Creed can tell the child immediately, "It was for us and for our salvation." If someone asks whether the virgin conception of Jesus really matters, the Christian who knows the creeds can immediately recall that, even for the earliest believers in Jesus, this was an essential doctrine.

HENDRICKSON PUBLISHERS   **ROSE** PUBLISHING

www.hendricksonrose.com

© 2009, 2015 Bristol Works, Inc.
Rose Publishing, LLC

Author: Benjamin Galan, MTS, ThM, Professor of Old Testament Hebrew and Literature.

Special thanks to Timothy Paul Jones, PhD, Southern Baptist Theological Seminary in Louisville, Kentucky; and Paul Carden, Executive Director, Centers for Apologetics Research (CFAR).

Note: The text of the Apostles' Creed and the Nicene Creed were modified from Creeds of Christendom, Vol. 1 by Philip Schaff.

Printed in the United States of America. 050518SCG

RELIGION/Biblical Studies/General

ISBN 978-1-59636-348-9

9 781596 363489

Stock #726X *The Creeds* pamphlet
Retailers: Package of 5 pamphlets = Stock #727X (ISBN: 978-159636-349-6)

HERESY	SUMMARY	COMMENTS
DOCETISM First Century	This heresy denies the reality of Jesus' human nature. Jesus only *appeared* to be human. (The word *docetism* is derived from a Greek word meaning "appearance.") Docetism was imported directly from Gnosticism into Christianity.	Today many people deny Jesus' divinity and consider him *just* a human. But Christians who focus only on Jesus' divinity and ignore the physical reality of Jesus' resurrection fall into a mild form of docetism.
EBIONITISM First Century	Ebionites denied Jesus' divinity and proposed the full continuity of the Old Testament Law. In other words, Christians should still submit to the Old Testament Law. Ebionites rejected Paul's teachings.	This heresy is significant because it prompted the church to define itself as distinct from Judaism, though still connected to the Old Testament.
ADOPTIONISM Second Century	Adoptionism claims that Jesus was born as (only) a human. Later, he became divine when God *adopted* him. This common position among Gnostics is a form of *Monarchianism*.	The Bible clearly shows that Jesus *is* God. Adoptionism arises from a misplaced respect for God's uniqueness. The idea that God became human is very difficult to understand. Today, some scholars still teach adoptionism as a way to understand Jesus as a human being who became divine in a *metaphorical* way.
MANICHEANISM Second Century	A heresy fusing Christian, Zoroastrian and Buddhist beliefs in a religion that was very popular and widespread until around the AD 600's. Mani called himself the *Paraclete* who would complete the work of people like Zoroaster, Plato, Buddha, and Jesus.	Manicheanism is important because it spread Gnosticism in the West and in Christianity (Augustine was a Manichean before becoming a Christian). Mani did not believe in a personal God; good and evil were equal but opposing forces.
MARCIONISM Second Century	Marcion made a radical break between Christianity and the Old Testament. Marcion proclaimed himself a follower of Jesus but rejected Paul's writings and anything that sounded like the Old Testament.	Today, many Christians who ignore the Old Testament are functional Marcionites. Whatever our doctrinal differences may be, the church confesses that the whole Bible, both Old and New Testaments, is the Word of God.
MODALISM Second Century	Modalism teaches that God takes on different modes of being at different times. In the Old testament God manifested himself as the Father. In the New Testament, God manifested himself as the Son. In the Church age, God manifests himself as the Holy Spirit.	Modalism attempts to make sense of the difficult doctrine of the Trinity. However, it is inconsistent with biblical testimony. Some people today continue to hold to a form of modalism. Though they identify themselves as Christians, they understand God in modalist terms.

HERESY	SUMMARY	COMMENTS
MONTANISM Second/Third Century	Montanists emphasized the spiritual gift of prophecy. Montanus, the founder, believed he received direct revelation from God through the Holy Spirit. Church fathers were divided concerning his teachings. However, Montanus's followers were more radical, claiming their prophecies were superior to the Bible. They also identified their three leaders with the Father, the Son, and the Holy Spirit. The church condemned their teachings and their legalistic way of life.	This heresy reminds us of the importance of the Holy Spirit. It also warns us of the excesses of some prophetic claims. Some Christians believe the Holy Spirit continues to give the gift of prophecy in our times. However, such prophecy must depend on biblical revelation to be valid.
APOLLINARIANISM Fourth Century	The idea that Jesus had a full human body and soul, but no human reason. Instead, the divine *logos* was Jesus' rationality. Apollinaris, Bishop of Laodicea, could not understand the union of two very different natures, human and divine. He attempted to preserve the divine glory by separating the human and the divine.	This view is based on a semi-Gnostic understanding of reality: the "soul" is good; the "material world" is bad. A rejection of the world as God's good creation can lead one to this position.
ARIANISM Fourth Century	Arianism argues that Jesus does not share the same *essence* with God, and thus does not share in the same divine nature with eternity and authority. The Nicene, Chalcedonian, and Athanasian Creeds are primarily responses to this heresy.	This heresy prompted the church to define its understanding of Christ. The question of Jesus' nature, divine or not, is directly related to his work of salvation.
MACEDONIANISM Fourth Century	A heresy similar to Arianism, also denying that Jesus is the same essence of God the Father, although affirming Jesus as eternal. In addition, believers denied the divinity of the Holy Spirit.	Despite the strong condemnation from the Nicaea Council, the rise of this heresy shows the extension and powerful effect of the Arian heresy in Christianity. It extended the doubts from the nature of Jesus to the nature of the Holy Spirit.
PELAGIANISM Fourth Century	Pelagius taught that sin had not affected human nature at all. Adam's sin set a "bad example," which people choose to follow or not. Christ came to offer a "good example" of life. Salvation means choosing to follow Jesus' example.	Pelagianism represents a conscious rejection of God's grace-filled action to save humans and reconcile people with himself. A milder form, called semi-Pelagianism, suggests that we cooperate with God for our justification.
NESTORIANISM Fifth Century	Nestorius attempted to explain Jesus' incarnation by suggesting that Jesus has two separate natures: a human and a divine nature. However, the separation is so extreme that it would appear that Jesus had both two natures and two persons: a divine nature for one "person" and a human one for another "person."	Nestorianism was a reaction to the teaching that Jesus had only one nature (Apollinarianism is an example of this teaching). This teaching caused a great split in Christianity.

THE NICENE CREED

The greatest doctrinal challenge to the church arose internally. Arius, a priest in Alexandria, suggested that if God begat Jesus, then Jesus had an origin. As such, Jesus did not share in the same divine essence with the Father. Therefore, Jesus was a lesser god.

In AD 325, Constantine called the leaders of the church to participate in a council—that is, an assembly of bishops. They met in the city of Nicaea, in present-day Turkey. The Council of Nicaea, made up of about 300 participants, overwhelmingly voted against the Arian teachings—ancient documents suggest that only three bishops refused to sign their agreement. The council expressed its views about God, Jesus, and the church in the Nicene Creed.

NICENE CREED	MEANING
We believe in one God, the Father Almighty, Maker *of heaven and earth, and* **of all things visible and invisible.**	As in the Apostles' Creed, the foundation of the Christian faith is the uniqueness of God. He alone is God. The Father is a distinct person, or individual reality, within the Godhead. In addition, God create *all* things. He is not created, but the Creator.
And in one Lord Jesus Christ, *the only-begotten* **Son of God, begotten of the Father** *before all worlds,* **Light of Light, very God of very God, begotten, not made, being of one substance with the Father; by whom all things were made;**	The creed affirms Jesus' • Lordship: The same title applied to God the Father the Old Testament. • Equality: Jesus is as much God as the Father. They share the same divine *essence.* Thus, Jesus is eternal. • Distinctness: Although they share the same essen Jesus is a *person* distinct from the Father.
Who for us, and for our salvation, came down *from heaven,* and was **incarnate** *by the Holy Ghost of the Virgin Mary,* and was made man; *he was crucified for us under Pontius Pilate,* and suffered, *and was buried,* and the third day he rose again, *according to the Scriptures,* and ascended into heaven, *and sits on the right hand of the Father;* from thence he shall come *again,* with glory, to judge the living and the dead; *whose kingdom shall have no end.*	The creed emphasizes both Jesus' divinity and humanity. • The image of coming down from heaven shows his divinity. • His miraculous virgin birth shows his humanity. • His suffering and death on the cross, again, show his full humanity. • His resurrection and ascension show his perfect work of salvation on behalf of humanity. • His final judgment shows his authority over the whole creation.
And in the Holy Spirit, *the Lord and Giver of life, who proceeds from the Father, who with the Father and the Son together is worshiped and glorified, who spoke by the prophets.*	The creed confirms the Bible's doctrine of the Trinit The Holy Spirit is fully divine, of the same *essence* a the Father and the Son, and is a distinct person wit the Godhead. In the sixth century, Western churches added "who proceeds from the Father *and the Son.*" It is this last addition, known as the *filioque* (Latin for "and the Son") that has caused division and conflict betwee the Eastern Orthodox and Western churches.
In one holy catholic and apostolic church; we acknowledge one baptism for the remission of sins; we look for the resurrection of the dead, and the life of the world to come. Amen. *[NOTE: The words in italics were added after the First Council of Nicaea in AD 325. The Council of Constantinople made these additions in AD 381.]*	One of the main purposes of the creed was to promote the unity of all believers in one universal church within the Apostolic tradition. Baptism represents this unity, as does the forgiveness of sins, the resurrection, and the world to come. These are all promises and hopes that link all Christians everywhere and at every time.

A CHRISTIAN EMPIRE In AD 313, Constantine became the sole ruler of the Roman Empire. His Edict of Milan, put into effect in 313, granted full tolerance to all religions of the Empire. Constantine fought hard to gain stability for the Empire. Scholars have debated much whether Constantine really converted to Christianity—and if so, at what age he did. Whatever the case, Constantine became the protector and, in time, promoter of Christianity throughout the Empire.

During Constantine's reign, the Arian controversy threatened to divide Christianity and bring chaos to the Empire. Constantine understood that a divided Christianity would also divide the Empire. To keep his Empire together, he needed to keep Christianity together. From a political standpoint, the Nicaea Council solved and prevented a schism in Christianity and the Roman Empire.

COMMENTS

Gnosticism, the God of the Bible is just the *miurge*, an evil god who brought about the aterial world. This god is himself created.

the New Testament, Jesus' Lordship is rectly connected to his divinity. He is not Lord mply because he earned it; rather, he is Lord cause he is God. Arius tried to understand the carnation, but his approach ignores the broad ntext of the Scriptures.

eresies about Jesus denied either his full vinity or his full humanity.
Denying Jesus' divinity removes his ability to save humanity from sin and death. Jesus is reduced to being a *model* of perfection.
Denying Jesus' humanity removes his ability to ntercede and represent humanity in his death.

e natural consequence of denying Jesus' vinity is that the Holy Spirit is not divine ther. After the creed of AD 325, the heresy out the Holy Spirit arose as a follow-up Arianism.

e Arian controversy threatened to split the ung and growing church. The creed allows the ssibility of unity of belief and practice. The rd *catholic* means "universal," in the sense of e whole world. It refers, then, to the worldwide lowship of all believers.

ATHANASIUS AND THE TRINITY

Athanasius was one of the most active opponents of Arius' teachings. His persistence and clear mind helped the church to clarify its positions and write it in a creed, the Nicene Creed.

Athanasius' teachings are summarized in the Athanasian Creed. While it is likely that Athanasius did not write it, the creed contains his teachings and main ideas. The Athanasian Creed begins by affirming, "This is what the catholic [or universal] faith teaches: we worship one God in the Trinity and the Trinity in unity. We distinguish among the persons, but we do not divide the substance [or essence]." After unpacking these ideas, the creed concludes, "So that in all things, as aforesaid, the Unity in Trinity and the Trinity in Unity is to be worshipped."

THE CHALCEDONIAN CREED

Map of Constantinopolis (Istanbul), printed in 1572 © Nikolay Staykov

Understanding the incarnation of Jesus—the embodiment of God the Son in human flesh—was one of the greatest challenges for the early church. In AD 451 the Council of Chalcedon (located in today's Turkey) provided a clear statement of the Apostolic teachings concerning Jesus. The Chalcedonian Creed made it clear that Jesus is fully God and fully human, two natures existing in perfect harmony in one person.

HERESIES TODAY

Many heresies—wrong beliefs—relate to two central biblical teachings: the Trinity and the Incarnation. Misunderstanding who God is will lead to misunderstanding what God has done and will do. Knowing the basic teachings of the church will help us identify and respond to heresies still existing today. The following chart provides some basic points to keep in mind about how ancient heresies show up today and what the correct, biblical teachings are.

ANCIENT HERESY	WHAT IT LOOKS LIKE TODAY
GNOSTICISM	• Confusing God with his creation. Taking things and people as part of the divine. • Rejecting the physical world as evil. • Belief that salvation is inside every person. • Speaking about Jesus as a guru or only as a "great teacher." • "Pop spirituality" based on Gnostic ideas. *The Secret, The Power of Now*, and many self-help teachings fall into this category.
MARCIONISM	• Rejecting the Old Testament. • Rejecting anything that sounds too Jewish fro the New Testament. • Completely divorcing the Old Testament from the New Testament.
MONARCHIANISM	• Denying the Trinity. • Claiming one god with three functions: First appearing as Father, then as Son, and now as Holy Spirit. • Both forms are active: Adoptionism and Modalism.
ARIANISM APOLLINARIANISM DOCETISM MACEDONIANISM NESTORIANISM	• Claims that Jesus was human only and became divine. • Claims that Jesus was only divine and merely appeared human. • Claims that Jesus was two persons with two natures in one being.
MONTANISM	• Offering prophecy beyond what the Bible reveals. • Claiming greater authority than the Bible. • Making the Holy Spirit more important than Jesus. • Using prophetic gifts to abuse other Christia trust and faith. • Misleading people through unverifiable prophecies.